MELISSA JOHNSON
50 Coffee Facts

Copyright © 2025 by Melissa Johnson

All rights reserved. No part of this publication may be reproduced, stored or transmitted in any form or by any means, electronic, mechanical, photocopying, recording, scanning, or otherwise without written permission from the publisher. It is illegal to copy this book, post it to a website, or distribute it by any other means without permission.

Melissa Johnson asserts the moral right to be identified as the author of this work.

Melissa Johnson has no responsibility for the persistence or accuracy of URLs for external or third-party Internet Websites referred to in this publication and does not guarantee that any content on such Websites is, or will remain, accurate or appropriate.

Designations used by companies to distinguish their products are often claimed as trademarks. All brand names and product names used in this book and on its cover are trade names, service marks, trademarks and registered trademarks of their respective owners. The publishers and the book are not associated with any product or vendor mentioned in this book. None of the companies referenced within the book have endorsed the book.

First edition

This book was professionally typeset on Reedsy.
Find out more at reedsy.com

"I have measured out my life with coffee spoons."

T.S. Eliot

Contents

Introduction		1
1	Chapter 1: History of Coffee	5
2	Chapter 2: Growing and Harvesting Coffee Beans	10
3	Chapter 3: Brewing Methods	15
4	Chapter 4: Coffee and Health	20
5	Chapter 5: Coffee Consumption	25
6	Conclusion	30
References		33

Introduction

Picture this: You've just woken up, the morning sun is creeping through the window, and the scent of freshly brewed coffee fills the air. You take that first sip—rich, bold, slightly bitter—and the world begins to come alive. It's not just a beverage; it's a ritual. It's a moment of solace before the chaos of the day begins. Coffee has that magical ability, doesn't it? To comfort, energize, and spark conversation.

For many of us, coffee is more than just a drink. It's an obsession. A passion. A gateway to connection, creativity, and a tiny moment of daily luxury. Whether you're sipping a perfectly crafted espresso, lounging with a cappuccino, or diving into a latte, coffee has a story. And it's a story that spans centuries, continents, and cultures.

This book is an invitation to explore that story—a peek into the fascinating world of coffee. Here, you'll discover 50 unique and compelling facts that I hope will both surprise and delight you. From the origins of the coffee bean to the health benefits (yes, they exist!), and from the secrets of brewing methods to the global impact of coffee consumption, this is your coffee lover's guide.

But before we dive into the details, let's set the stage a bit more.

You see, coffee isn't just something you drink; it's a cultural phenomenon. The rich history of coffee stretches all the way back to the 15th century, when the first coffee beans were cultivated in Ethiopia. Legends surround the discovery of coffee—one of the most popular being the story of Kaldi, a goat herder who noticed his flock of goats dancing after nibbling on a certain berry. Whether myth or truth, it's clear: coffee has always had an almost mystical allure.

Why did I write this book? Simple. Like you, I've been drawn into the world of coffee with an unrelenting curiosity. Over the years, I've worked and sat in coffee shops around the world, brewed countless cups, explored every nook and cranny of the coffee universe, and marveled at how this humble bean has shaped cultures and changed lives. Coffee is no longer just a drink you grab on your way to work—it's an art form, a science, and a source of community.

We'll begin by taking a journey through the *history of coffee*. We'll explore where it all started, the evolution of coffee culture, and how the coffee bean made its way around the world, influencing societies along the way.

Next, we'll dive into the *growing and harvesting of coffee beans*. You might not realize it, but the process is intricate, full of nuances that make all the difference in the final cup you drink. From the altitude at which the beans are grown to the way they're harvested and processed, every step in the supply chain impacts the flavor, aroma, and body of your coffee.

Then, we'll talk about the magic behind *brewing methods*. From the classic drip coffee maker to the precision of pour-over and the intensity of French press, there's a method for every coffee lover. We'll explore how different techniques unlock the hidden flavors of your beans, and why sometimes, the simplest methods produce the most satisfying results.

You might be surprised to learn that coffee isn't just a pick-me-up; it has real *health benefits* too. In our chapter on coffee and health, we'll dive into the research behind coffee's positive effects—from improving brain function to potentially reducing the risk of certain diseases.

Finally, we'll explore *coffee consumption*. It's a fascinating topic—how coffee trends shift across cultures, how coffee impacts global economies, and what drives the current coffee boom we're seeing today. Whether you're a casual drinker or a full-blown coffee connoisseur, this chapter will offer you new perspectives on your daily brew.

This book isn't just for the coffee expert; it's for anyone who has ever taken a sip of their favorite brew and thought, *What's the story behind this cup?* Whether you're a seasoned coffee aficionado or a newcomer, there's something in here for everyone. Each fact is designed to expand your appreciation for this beloved beverage and enhance the experience of every cup you drink.

As you turn these pages, I encourage you to savor each fact, to ponder the rich history behind every bean, and to think about the art and science that goes into making your perfect cup. By the end of this book, you'll not only be a smarter coffee drinker—you'll be a coffee lover with a deeper understanding of the magic behind every sip.

So, let's dive in. Grab your favorite mug, take a seat, and let's explore the world of coffee like never before.

1

Chapter 1: History of Coffee

C offee's journey from a humble berry to the global beverage we know today is a fascinating tale. From the legendary discovery of coffee in Ethiopia to its rise as a global commodity, the history of coffee is rich with intrigue, innovation, and cultural shifts. Let's explore 10 essential facts that chart coffee's historic path.

1. **The Legend of Kaldi and the Discovery of Coffee.** One of the earliest legends of coffee dates back to the 9th century in Ethiopia. Kaldi, a goat herder, noticed that his goats became unusually energetic after eating red berries from a particular tree.

Curious, he tried the berries himself and experienced a burst of energy. He shared his discovery with a local monk, who found that brewing the berries helped him stay awake during long prayer sessions. The magic of coffee was born.

2. **Coffee's Journey to the Arabian Peninsula.** By the 15th century, coffee spread from Ethiopia to Yemen, where it began to take its modern form. Yemeni traders established coffee plantations, and by the 1500s, coffee had become a central part of Islamic culture. Coffeehouses, known as *qahveh khaneh*, flourished, becoming places of conversation, intellectual exchange, and entertainment—important cultural hubs in the Middle East.

3. **Coffee Reaches the Ottoman Empire.** Coffee's popularity surged in the Ottoman Empire during the 16th century. In Istanbul, coffeehouses became the epicenter of social and political life. Sultan Suleiman the Magnificent passed a law that regulated the preparation and serving of coffee, cementing its place in Ottoman society. This development ensured coffee's status as a symbol of hospitality and culture throughout the empire.

4. **Coffee Arrives in Europe.** Coffee spread to Europe in the 16th century as the Turkish Army invaded Vienna, leaving behind bags of coffee when they fled. In 1650, the first British coffeehouse opened in Oxford, England, under the name "The Angel." The venue became a center for academic and intellectual discussions, earning the nickname "penny universities" because you could buy a cup of coffee for a penny and engage in stimulating conversation with scholars. Coffeehouses continued to spread throughout Europe, influencing politics, literature, and social life.

5. **The Birth of the Coffee Trade.** In the 1600s, European colonial powers began establishing coffee plantations in tropical regions. The Dutch were the first to successfully cultivate coffee outside of Arabia, introducing it to Java (now Indonesia). The French

and Portuguese followed suit, bringing coffee to colonies in the Caribbean, South America, and Africa. By the 1700s, coffee had become one of the world's most valuable traded commodities.

6. **The French Revolution and Coffee's Role in Society.** During the French Revolution, coffeehouses played a pivotal role in the political upheaval. Revolutionary leaders and philosophers frequently gathered in Parisian coffeehouses to discuss ideas, strategies, and critiques of the monarchy. The social setting encouraged free speech, debate, and the exchange of revolutionary ideas, making coffee a symbol of intellectual rebellion.

7. **The Birth of the Coffeehouse Culture in America.** The first American coffeehouse, *The Tontine Coffee House*, opened in New York City in 1792. It quickly became a hub for business and social gatherings, where deals were made and news was shared. As coffeehouses continued to open in major cities, they became a cornerstone of early American life—venues where politicians, writers, and artists could gather and exchange ideas.

8. **The Rise of Instant Coffee.** In 1890 New Zealander David Stang created a 'soluble instant coffee' followed by Japanese chemist Satori Kato in 1901 inventing a method close to what we know today for creating instant coffee. The invention was a game-changer, providing a quick, convenient way to enjoy coffee without brewing. During World War I and II, instant coffee became a staple for soldiers, solidifying its place in global coffee culture. Today, it remains a go-to option for those seeking speed and simplicity.

9. **The Coffee Boom of the 1990s.** The 1990s saw an explosion in coffee consumption, driven by the rise of specialty coffee shops. Chains like Starbucks made high-quality coffee drinks accessible to the masses, sparking an interest in espresso-based beverages such as lattes, cappuccinos, and mochas. The "third wave coffee movement" emerged, emphasizing artisanal, single-origin beans

and sustainable practices, which transformed how coffee was produced, brewed, and enjoyed.
10. **The Modern Coffee Revolution and Sustainability.** Today, coffee is more than just a drink—it's a global industry valued at over $100 billion. With growing concerns about the environment and fair trade practices, sustainability has become a core focus of the coffee industry. Companies are increasingly committed to sourcing beans responsibly, supporting farmers with fair wages, and reducing the environmental impact of coffee production. The modern coffee revolution continues, blending rich history with forward-thinking innovation.

Chapter 2: Growing and Harvesting Coffee Beans

CHAPTER 2: GROWING AND HARVESTING COFFEE BEANS

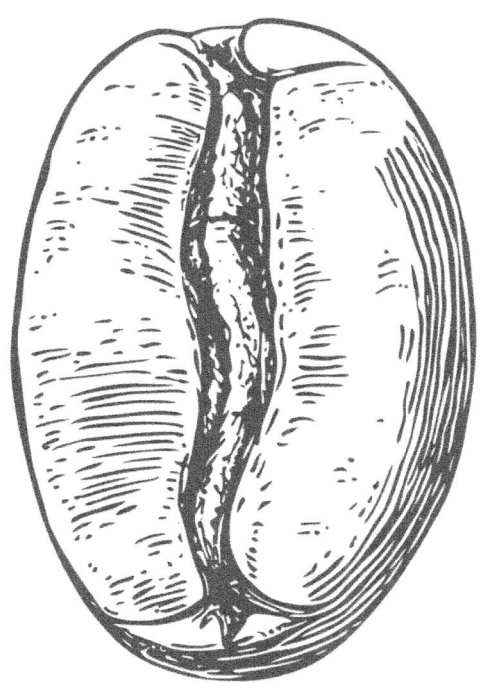

Coffee isn't just a product of a magical bean—it's the result of a carefully controlled agricultural process that requires precision, patience, and a bit of luck. The journey from seed to brew involves several stages, each of which impacts the final flavor of your coffee. Let's explore 10 essential facts about how coffee is grown, harvested, and prepared for your cup.

1. **The Coffee Belt: Where Coffee Grows.** Coffee is grown in a region known as the *coffee belt*, which lies between the Tropic of Cancer and the Tropic of Capricorn. This zone includes parts of Central and South America, sub-Saharan Africa, Southeast Asia,

and Oceania. The consistent climate in this belt—moderate temperatures, ample rainfall, and rich soil—provides ideal conditions for coffee plants to thrive.

2. **Arabica vs. Robusta: The Two Main Coffee Varieties.** There are two main species of coffee beans: *Arabica* and *Robusta*. Arabica beans are grown at higher altitudes and are known for their smooth, complex flavors, often with hints of fruit or floral notes. Robusta beans, grown at lower elevations, are stronger, more bitter, and contain more caffeine. Arabica beans dominate the global coffee market, but Robusta beans are crucial for certain blends and espresso.

3. **The Role of Altitude in Flavor.** The altitude at which coffee is grown plays a significant role in its flavor profile. Coffee grown at higher elevations—between 3,000 and 6,000 feet—is often more acidic and complex. The cooler temperatures slow the coffee plant's growth, which allows the beans to develop more nuanced flavors. Lower-altitude beans, in contrast, tend to be less acidic and have a more straightforward, bolder taste.

4. **Coffee Trees: Perennial Plants That Take Time to Mature.** Unlike most crops that are planted annually, coffee trees are perennial plants, meaning they live for many years. However, it takes time for them to mature. A coffee tree usually begins to produce fruit after 3 to 4 years and reaches full production potential after 5 to 6 years. This long maturation period is one reason why coffee is such a labor-intensive crop to cultivate.

5. **The Coffee Cherry: Not Just a Bean.** The coffee "bean" you enjoy is actually the seed of a fruit called the coffee cherry. These cherries begin as small green fruits that ripen to a bright red (or sometimes yellow or purple) color when they're ready for harvest. Each cherry contains two seeds—these are the coffee beans we roast and brew. In some regions, the cherries may contain only

one bean, known as a "peaberry."

6. **When Is Coffee Harvested?** Coffee cherries are typically harvested once a year, though this can vary based on the region and climate. In tropical climates, some areas experience multiple harvests throughout the year, while others have a single annual harvest. The ripening process of the cherries is gradual, and picking must be done carefully—usually by hand—to ensure that only ripe cherries are harvested, as unripe cherries can negatively affect flavor.

7. **Selective vs. Strip Harvesting.** There are two main methods of harvesting coffee cherries: *selective picking* and *strip picking*. Selective picking is the more labor-intensive method, where workers pick only the ripe cherries from each tree, ensuring that the coffee is of higher quality. Strip picking, on the other hand, involves stripping all cherries from the branch at once, regardless of ripeness. While faster and more cost-effective, strip picking often results in lower-quality coffee.

8. **Processing Coffee: Wet vs. Dry Method.** Once harvested, coffee cherries must be processed to extract the beans. There are two primary methods: the *wet method* and the *dry method*. In the wet method, the cherries are pulped to remove the outer skin, and the beans are then fermented to remove the mucilage before drying. In the dry method, the entire cherry is sun-dried before being hulled to extract the beans. Each method imparts different flavors to the beans, with the wet method generally producing cleaner, brighter flavors.

9. **The Importance of Proper Drying.** After processing, the beans must be dried to about 10-12% moisture content to prevent mold and spoilage during storage. This is a delicate process that requires careful attention. Beans are often spread out in the sun on drying patios or raised beds, where they're turned regularly to ensure

even drying. In regions with unpredictable weather, mechanical dryers are used to speed up the process. Improper drying can lead to uneven flavors and poor-quality coffee.

10. **Harvesting and Sustainability: The Future of Coffee Farming.** As climate change poses an increasing threat to coffee-growing regions, sustainability has become a crucial focus for farmers and the coffee industry. Many coffee producers are adopting environmentally friendly practices, such as using shade-grown coffee techniques, which preserve biodiversity and reduce the need for chemical fertilizers. Additionally, fair-trade certifications and direct trade relationships are helping improve the livelihoods of coffee farmers while ensuring better quality beans for consumers.

3

Chapter 3: Brewing Methods

B rewing coffee is both an art and a science. Whether you're crafting a delicate pour-over or brewing a bold espresso shot, each method extracts different flavors from the coffee beans. In this chapter, we'll explore 10 essential facts about the most popular brewing methods and how they affect the taste, aroma, and experience of your cup.

1. **Drip Coffee: The Classic Standby.** The drip coffee maker is the most common brewing method in American households. It works by heating water and allowing it to drip through a filter filled with ground coffee. The result is a clean, mild cup with a

smooth flavor. Drip coffee is easy to make, but the quality can vary based on factors like water temperature and the grind size of the coffee beans.

2. **French Press: Full-Bodied and Bold.** The French press (or *press pot*) is known for producing a full-bodied, robust cup of coffee. It uses a simple method: coarsely ground coffee is steeped in hot water for about four minutes before being pressed through a metal filter. This method allows the oils and fine particles from the coffee grounds to remain in the brew, giving it a rich, creamy texture and deep flavor.

3. **Pour-Over: Precision Brewing.** Pour-over brewing is a hands-on method that gives you full control over the brewing process. Ground coffee is placed in a filter, and hot water is poured slowly over the grounds in a circular motion. The most common pour-over devices are the Chemex and the V60. This method allows for greater precision in water temperature and flow rate, resulting in a clean, complex cup of coffee with bright flavors.

4. **Espresso: Intense and Concentrated.** Espresso is the base for many popular coffee drinks, including lattes, cappuccinos, and Americanos. To make espresso, finely ground coffee is tightly packed into a portafilter, and hot water is forced through the grounds under high pressure. The result is a small but intense shot of coffee with a thick crema on top. Espresso is prized for its rich flavor and concentrated aroma, making it the perfect base for milk-based drinks.

5. **AeroPress: Portable and Versatile.** The AeroPress is a relatively new but highly popular brewing method, known for its versatility and ease of use. It works by steeping coffee grounds in hot water for a short time (about 30 seconds to 1 minute) before pressing the coffee through a filter using a plunger. The result is a smooth, low-acid cup with a slightly stronger taste than a pour-over, and

the AeroPress is beloved for its portability, making it a great option for travel.

6. **Cold Brew: Smooth and Sweet.** Cold brew coffee is made by steeping coarsely ground coffee beans in cold water for an extended period, usually 12 to 24 hours. This slow extraction process produces a coffee that's smoother and less acidic than traditional hot brewed coffee. Cold brew is often served over ice, making it perfect for hot weather. It's also highly concentrated, so it can be diluted with water, milk, or cream to taste.

7. **Moka Pot: Italian Classic.** The Moka pot, often called a stovetop espresso maker, is a popular Italian method for brewing strong, espresso-like coffee at home. It consists of two chambers: one for water and the other for ground coffee. When heated, water is forced through the grounds into the top chamber, producing a rich, intense brew. While not technically espresso, the Moka pot produces a bold, full-bodied coffee that's perfect for those who enjoy a strong cup.

8. **Siphon: The Coffee Lover's Showpiece.** The siphon coffee maker, also known as a vacuum pot, is a visually striking brewing method that uses vapor pressure and vacuum to brew coffee. Water is heated in the lower chamber, creating pressure that forces it into the upper chamber containing the coffee grounds. After steeping, the coffee returns to the lower chamber as it cools. The siphon method produces a clean, aromatic cup with bright flavors, and it's often used as a showpiece in coffee shops due to its dramatic brewing process.

9. **Turkish Coffee: Traditional and Rich.** Turkish coffee is one of the oldest methods of brewing, known for its strong, rich flavor and unique preparation. Finely ground coffee is combined with water and sugar (optional) in a small pot called a *cezve* and heated over low heat until it begins to foam. The coffee is then served

unfiltered, allowing the fine coffee grounds to settle at the bottom of the cup. It's typically enjoyed with a glass of water and sweet treats, often in social settings.

10. **Percolator: Old-School and Strong.** The percolator was once the standard coffee-brewing method in many households, especially in the mid-20th century. It works by cycling boiling water through coffee grounds repeatedly until the desired strength is reached. The result is a bold, sometimes bitter cup of coffee. While percolators have largely fallen out of favor, they are still loved by those who enjoy a strong, traditional brew. The method can be a bit over-extracted if not carefully monitored, but it can produce a powerful cup of coffee.

4

Chapter 4: Coffee and Health

CHAPTER 4: COFFEE AND HEALTH

C offee isn't just a morning pick-me-up; it's packed with potential health benefits. From boosting brain function to supporting heart health, coffee can be a key player in your overall wellness. Like all things, coffee can have adverse effects in high quantities and it's important to acknowledge that it should be consumed in moderation. In this chapter, we'll explore 10 fascinating facts about the health benefits of coffee and how enjoying your daily cup might do more for you than you think.

1. **Improves Cognitive Function.** Coffee is known to improve brain function by stimulating the central nervous system. Caffeine,

the main active ingredient in coffee, increases alertness, enhances focus, and improves reaction time. Studies show that regular coffee consumption may even help protect against neurodegenerative diseases like Alzheimer's and Parkinson's, as caffeine has been shown to reduce the buildup of certain proteins linked to these conditions.

2. **Boosts Physical Performance.** Caffeine is a natural performance booster. It has been shown to increase adrenaline levels and break down fat cells, making fatty acids available for energy during physical activities. This can lead to improved endurance and strength. Studies suggest that consuming coffee before a workout can increase performance, helping athletes push harder and recover faster. It's no wonder many fitness enthusiasts swear by their pre-workout cup of coffee.

3. **Rich in Antioxidants.** Coffee is one of the largest sources of antioxidants in the Western diet. Antioxidants help combat oxidative stress and inflammation in the body, which are linked to various chronic diseases, including cancer and heart disease, making it a powerhouse of health benefits when consumed in moderation.

4. **May Lower the Risk of Type 2 Diabetes.** Drinking coffee may help reduce the risk of developing type 2 diabetes. Studies have shown that regular coffee consumption is associated with a decreased risk of this chronic condition. The exact mechanism isn't entirely understood, but researchers believe that the antioxidants and anti-inflammatory compounds in coffee may improve insulin sensitivity and protect the body's ability to regulate blood sugar.

5. **Supports Liver Health.** Your liver can benefit from your daily coffee habit. Studies suggest that coffee drinkers have a lower risk of liver diseases, including cirrhosis and liver cancer. The compounds in coffee may help prevent the accumulation of

fat in the liver and reduce inflammation. Additionally, coffee consumption has been linked to a decreased risk of liver fibrosis, a condition where scar tissue builds up in the liver.

6. **May Protect Against Depression.** Coffee has been shown to have mood-boosting effects. Some studies suggest that regular coffee consumption may reduce the risk of depression. The caffeine in coffee increases the production of certain neurotransmitters like serotonin, dopamine, and noradrenaline, which are responsible for regulating mood and emotions. Drinking coffee may help keep your mood lifted and your mind sharp.

7. **Can Aid in Weight Loss.** Caffeine, the main stimulant in coffee, is often included in weight loss supplements due to its ability to boost metabolism. Drinking coffee can increase calorie burning and fat oxidation, particularly when consumed in the morning. In addition to stimulating fat loss, coffee can help suppress appetite for a short time, making it easier to stick to a calorie-controlled diet.

8. **May Lower the Risk of Certain Cancers.** Regular coffee consumption has been linked to a decreased risk of certain types of cancer, including colorectal, liver, and breast cancer. The antioxidants and other bioactive compounds found in coffee may help protect cells from damage and inhibit the growth of cancerous cells. Although coffee isn't a cure for cancer, its health-promoting properties can contribute to a lower overall risk.

9. **Promotes Heart Health.** Coffee has long been thought to have negative effects on heart health, but recent studies suggest that moderate coffee consumption can actually benefit your cardiovascular system. Regular coffee drinkers have a lower risk of developing heart disease and stroke. The antioxidants in coffee may help reduce inflammation in the arteries, while caffeine can improve blood circulation and help regulate blood pressure. (done)

10. **Improves Longevity.** Believe it or not, drinking coffee might help you live longer. Multiple large-scale studies have found that coffee drinkers tend to live longer than those who abstain. The health benefits associated with coffee, such as reduced risk of chronic diseases like heart disease, diabetes, and certain cancers, may contribute to a longer life. Of course, moderation is key, but enjoying a cup of coffee each day could be one of the simplest ways to support longevity.

5

Chapter 5: Coffee Consumption

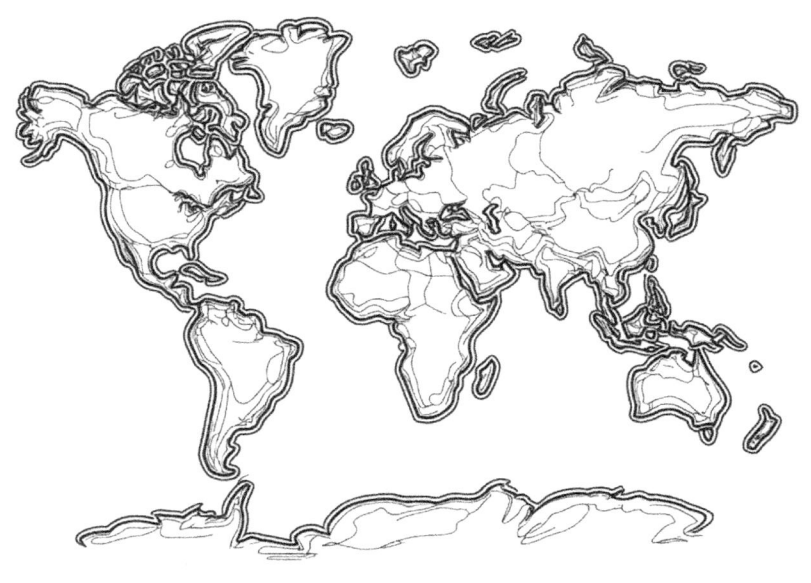

C offee is one of the most consumed beverages in the world, and its popularity spans continents, cultures, and cuisines. Whether enjoyed in a bustling café or brewed at home, coffee plays a vital role in daily life for millions of people. This chapter explores 10 fascinating facts about coffee consumption across the globe.

1. **Finland: The Coffee Capital.** Finland holds the title for the world's highest per capita coffee consumption. On average, Finns drink around 9 - 12 kilograms of coffee per person per year,

equating to approximately four cups of coffee a day. The Finns prefer light-roast coffee and often enjoy it in a relaxed, social setting. Coffee is so central to Finnish culture that it's common to have coffee breaks known as "kahvitauko" in both work and social contexts.

2. **Italy: Espresso Culture.** In Italy, coffee isn't just a beverage; it's a culture. The espresso is the foundation of Italian coffee traditions, and it's consumed quickly—standing at the bar. Italians typically enjoy espresso in the morning, followed by cappuccino or macchiato. The art of making a great espresso is highly regarded, with each region offering its own take on the drink. Italian coffee culture emphasizes simplicity, quality, and the enjoyment of a fast-paced ritual.

3. **Turkey: Coffee as Tradition.** Turkish coffee is a deeply rooted tradition, famous for its strong, unfiltered brew served in small cups. It's made by boiling finely ground coffee beans with water and sugar in a special pot called a *cezve*. Turkish coffee is often accompanied by sweets and served during social gatherings or after meals. The method of preparation and its accompanying rituals have been recognized by UNESCO as an Intangible Cultural Heritage of Humanity since 2013.

4. **Sweden: Fika and Coffee Breaks.** In Sweden, coffee is more than just a drink—it's part of a daily ritual known as *fika*. Fika is the Swedish tradition of taking a coffee break, typically accompanied by pastries or sweets. It's a social experience, meant to foster connection and relaxation. The average Swede consumes around 6 - 8 kilograms of coffee per person per year, and coffee breaks are integrated into the workday and personal life, making it a cherished part of Swedish culture.

5. **Brazil: The World's Coffee Giant.** Brazil is the world's largest coffee producer, and it's also one of the top consumers of coffee.

Coffee is so integral to daily life that the average Brazilian drinks around 6.4kg of coffee per year. In Brazil, coffee is often served as *cafezinho*—a small, sweet cup of coffee served in a small glass. Brazilian coffee is typically stronger and sweeter than many other varieties, and it's a symbol of hospitality when visiting friends or family.

6. **Japan: Coffee with a Twist.** In Japan, coffee consumption is on the rise, with unique and innovative takes on traditional coffee drinks. The Japanese enjoy a wide variety of coffee styles, from canned coffee available in vending machines to meticulously brewed pour-overs. Coffee shops in Japan often offer quiet, cozy spaces where patrons can relax, and some even serve "specialty" cold brew coffees, offering a smooth, less acidic alternative to hot coffee. Japanese coffee culture is a blend of tradition and modernity.

7. **United States: A Diverse Coffee Landscape.** The United States is home to an incredibly diverse coffee culture. From large corporate chains like Starbucks to local, artisanal coffee roasters, the U.S. is a hub for coffee innovation. While drip coffee and espresso-based drinks dominate the market, there's also a growing interest in cold brew, nitro coffee, and single-origin brews. Coffee consumption varies widely, with some people preferring a quick, convenient cup from a drive-thru, while others seek a more nuanced, specialty coffee experience.

8. **Ethiopia: The Birthplace of Coffee.** In Ethiopia, coffee is not just a beverage; it's a sacred and cultural ritual. The country is considered the birthplace of coffee, and the coffee ceremony remains a fundamental part of Ethiopian life. The ceremony involves roasting green coffee beans, grinding them by hand, and brewing the coffee in a jebena (a traditional clay pot). Ethiopian coffee is often served with incense and accompanied by the sharing

of stories, making it a deeply communal and spiritual experience.
9. **Vietnam: Strong and Sweet.** Vietnam is the world's second-largest coffee exporter, and the Vietnamese take their coffee seriously. The most iconic drink in Vietnam is *cà phê sữa đá*—iced coffee served with sweetened condensed milk. The coffee is brewed using a traditional Vietnamese drip filter called a *phin*, which creates a strong, concentrated brew. Vietnam's coffee culture is deeply intertwined with its street food scene, with vendors offering rich, sweet coffee that's perfect for a hot, humid day.
10. **Australia: Flat White and Café Culture.** Australia has gained global recognition for its café culture, especially the flat white. The definition of a flat white seems to vary around the world but in Australia your order would arrive as an espresso with steamed milk and a small amount of foam. In Australia, coffee isn't just about the drink—it's about the experience. Coffee shops are central to urban life, offering a place for people to socialize, work, and relax. Australians take their coffee seriously, with an emphasis on high-quality beans and expertly brewed drinks.

6

Conclusion

CONCLUSION

As we've explored throughout this book, coffee is far more than just a beverage—it's a global tradition, a rich cultural experience, and a healthful companion that enhances both mind and body. From its fascinating history and complex growing processes to the diverse brewing methods and wide-reaching health benefits, coffee truly has something for everyone. It's a drink that transcends borders, connects cultures, and sparks moments of connection, relaxation, and inspiration.

Whether you're a casual coffee drinker or a dedicated enthusiast, there's always something new to discover about coffee. Perhaps you're now inspired to explore different brewing methods, experiment with new beans, or deepen your understanding of the health benefits this drink has to offer. Coffee's world is vast, and there's always more to learn and enjoy. The facts presented in this book are just the beginning of your coffee journey.

If you've enjoyed this book and learned something new along the way, I encourage you to share your thoughts and leave a review on Amazon. Your feedback not only helps me grow as a writer but also supports other coffee lovers in finding this book. Whether you're reflecting on your favorite coffee facts, or simply want to share how coffee fits into your daily routine, your review will help build a community of coffee enthusiasts around the globe.

So, next time you take that sip of your favorite brew, remember that you're part of a rich, vibrant tradition. Coffee connects us all—whether through its history, its health benefits, or the simple pleasure it brings to our lives. Keep exploring, keep savoring, and, most importantly, keep enjoying the perfect cup of coffee. Thank you for being part of this journey!

References

1. Britannica. (n.d.). *History of coffee*. Encyclopaedia Britannica. Retrieved January 24, 2025, from https://www.britannica.com/topic/history-of-coffee
2. Tinsley, A. (2021, July 22). *The evolution of the coffee house*. The Spruce Eats. Retrieved January 24, 2025, from https://www.thespruceeats.com/evolution-of-the-coffee-house-765825
3. Java Coffee. (n.d.). *History of Java coffee*. Specialty Coffee Association of Indonesia. Retrieved January 24, 2025, from https://specialtycoffee.id/java-coffee-history/
4. Nationwide Coffee. (2020, October 21). *The history of instant coffee*. Nationwide Coffee. Retrieved January 24, 2025, from https://www.nationwidecoffee.co.uk/news/the-history-of-instant-coffee#:~:text=In%201890%2C%20New%20Zealander%20David,was%20offered%20to%20the%20public.
5. **Perfect Daily Grind**. (2015, June 8). How does altitude affect coffee and its taste in the cup? *Perfect Daily Grind*. Retrieved January 24, 2025, from https://perfectdailygrind.com/2015/06/how-does-altitude-affect-coffee-and-its-taste-in-the-cup/#:~:text=The%20main%20reason%20that%20higher,little%20character%20in%20the%20cup.
6. **Perfect Daily Grind**. (2021, August 6). Why do coffee plants flower? What does it mean for producers? *Perfect Daily Grind*.

Retrieved January 24, 2025, from https://perfectdailygrind.com/2021/08/why-do-coffee-plants-flower-what-does-it-mean-for-producers/#:~:text=Coffee%20trees%20start%20to%20flower,a%20rich%20jasmine%2Dlike%20scent.
7. Espresso Coffee Guide. (n.d.). *Harvesting coffee*. Espresso Coffee Guide. Retrieved January 24, 2025, from https://espressocoffeeguide.com/all-about-coffee-2/harvesting-coffee/
8. Sweet Maria's. (2020, August). *Processing and drying of coffee – A review*. Sweet Maria's Library. Retrieved January 24, 2025, from https://library.sweetmarias.com/wp-content/uploads/2020/08/Processing-and-Drying-of-Coffee-%E2%80%93-A-Review.pdf
9. **Counter Culture Coffee**. (n.d.). *Coffee basics: Brewing methods*. Counter Culture Coffee. Retrieved January 24, 2025, from https://counterculturecoffee.com/blogs/counter-culture-coffee/coffee-basics-brewing-methods?srsltid=AfmBOopAqXV0-5ku2R4IaVXD7wf0TlzDn4UTfhWzk0h37hctGxt6YNIZ
10. World Siphonist Championship. (n.d.). *What is siphon coffee?* World Siphonist Championship. Retrieved January 24, 2025, from https://worldsiphonistchampionship.org/what-is-siphoncoffee/
11. Science ABC. (n.d.). *What is a coffee percolator and how does it work?* Science ABC. Retrieved January 24, 2025, from https://www.scienceabc.com/eyeopeners/what-is-a-coffee-percolator-and-how-does-it-work.html
12. **MDPI**. (2024). Coffee consumption and its health effects: A review of the literature. *Nutrients, 16*(24), 4257. https://doi.org/10.3390/nu16244257
13. Meamar, M., Raise-Abdullahi, P., Rashidy-Pour, A., & Raeis-Abdollahi, E. (2024). Coffee and mental disorders: How caffeine affects anxiety and depression. *Progress in Brain Research, 288*, 115-132. https://doi.org/10.1016/bs.pbr.2024.06.015
14. Raise-Abdullahi, P., Raeis-Abdollahi, E., Meamar, M., & Rashidy-

REFERENCES

Pour, A. (2024). Effects of coffee on cognitive function. *Progress in Brain Research, 288*, 133-166. https://doi.org/10.1016/bs.pbr.2024.06.016

15. **Alzheimer's Society**. (n.d.). Caffeine and dementia. *Alzheimer's Society*. Retrieved January 24, 2025, from https://www.alzheimers.org.uk/about-dementia/managing-the-risk-of-dementia/possible-risks-of-dementia/caffeine
16. Graham, T. E. (2001). Caffeine and exercise: Metabolism, endurance and performance. *Sports Medicine, 31*(11), 785-807. https://doi.org/10.2165/00007256-200131110-00002
17. **Healthline**. (2023, October 3). Coffee: The world's biggest source of antioxidants. *Healthline*. Retrieved January 24, 2025, from https://www.healthline.com/nutrition/coffee-worlds-biggest-source-of-antioxidants#benefits
18. **Diabetes.co.uk**. (n.d.). Coffee and diabetes. *Diabetes.co.uk*. Retrieved January 24, 2025, from https://www.diabetes.co.uk/food/coffee-and-diabetes.html#google_vignette
19. **British Liver Trust**. (n.d.). Coffee and liver health. *British Liver Trust*. Retrieved January 24, 2025, from https://britishlivertrust.org.uk/information-and-support/living-with-a-liver-condition/coffee/
20. **Cancer Research UK**. (2016, June 15). Coffee and cancer: What does the evidence say? *Cancer Research UK*. Retrieved January 24, 2025, from https://news.cancerresearchuk.org/2016/06/15/coffee-and-cancer-what-does-the-evidence-say/
21. **European Society of Cardiology**. (2023, October 10). Coffee drinking is associated with increased longevity. *European Society of Cardiology*. Retrieved January 24, 2025, from https://www.escardio.org/The-ESC/Press-Office/Press-releases/Coffee-drinking-is-associated-with-increased-longevity
22. **Anticosole Italy**. (n.d.). Understanding Italian coffee culture.

Anticosole Italy. Retrieved January 24, 2025, from https://anticosoleitaly.com/understanding-italian-coffee-culture/

23. OpenAI. (2025). *ChatGPT* (GPT-4-turbo). https://openai.com/chatgpt

Printed in Dunstable, United Kingdom